T

Stop the drama bus, I'm getting off.

A navigational guide to self empowerment

Trina A.L. Zacharias

ISBN: 1775080609
ISBN-13: 978-1775080602

DEDICATION

To my mother...
Who’s lessons have inspired my action

Trina A.L. Zacharias

TRANSIT SYSTEM

Trina A.L. Zacharias

THE DRIVER

I am the driver who will be guiding you though this journey on the drama bus. I do not claim to have any mental health training, nor do I hold a degree in any field. I truly believe that there is a need for mental health professionals, now more than ever. Knowing this, I felt compelled to write this workbook to empower others to take control of their own journey, all while being able to honor myself, my personal journey and the lessons I am so grateful to have learned.

I have been in the service industry, in various jobs and positions, for over 30 years and in management for over 25 years. Around 2010, I started struggling with my management style, as a new generation of employees was entering the workforce. My previous methods (see the manager manual chapter) and tactics were no longer working, and I had to quickly learn a new management style in order to continue with my career. I did extra studying on this generation and started modifying my approach through trial and error.

I had always wanted to write a book on choices and as I worked with these young adults, this motivation became stronger. As a young teen, I went through a sequence of events that led me to a group called Alateen. Alateen is a program designed for adolescents who are in need of recovery from another's addiction. The most impactful lesson I learned in this group was the power and wisdom of choice. I learned then that I had control over my life, the direction it took, and the consequences carried by my actions or inactions. This is a powerful lesson for a teenager to learn, and it is something I carry with me to this very day.

When I sat down to start writing about "choices" it was 2012, but the more I wrote the more I realized that it was missing a key element involving the ability to make choices. I scrapped that book a few years later, evolving it into what you are reading today. A simple practical navigational book to guide you to a place of empowerment through the ability to make independent choices, and a place where it is okay to make the mistakes needed to learn lessons.

As a parent of one of these new generational individuals and as a manager who works daily with them, I have been placed in a unique position to study and interact with thousands of younger people. In my industry, there is very high turnover. This is due in part to the nature of the industry, but is more frequently due to the quality of the relationships employees build in the workplace. I have been fortunate to maintain a low rate of turnover, and know that this is thanks in part to using the skills I now wish to impart to you.

Though I have seen success using these skills as a parent and as an employer, I have only included these as sub-sections at the end of the book. This was done intentionally, as the only place to start with any new skill is with the self. This guide book is intended for everyone, regardless of if you are a teenager, a parent, a mentor, or a grandparent... I wish you the same enlightenment and empowerment I found all those years ago.

Now that we've decided on a route destination, let's get this bus moving...

ROUTES AND STOPS

1 THE DRAMA BUS

Today, North America is fueled by emotions (judgment, fear, worry, happiness, sorrow, anger, delight, and regret). Take a look at our media: our reality shows, our social media, our dirty laundry. A constant supply of emotional stimulation with each success and failure we experience, or see others experience, on display, whether in our personal or professional life. Even in consumer marketing, 80% of all purchase decisions are made with emotions, and only 20% with logic.

This conditioning has been integrated gradually and has evolved with each passing generation. The degree of drama this has created in our lives you may find seriously surprising and possibly a little shocking. Breaking free of this behavior will be one of the most enlightening and difficult journeys you will ever undertake, but the personal awareness and wisdom you will gain will change your life forever.

Drama in our personal life takes many forms, like gossip, observation, judgment of others, assumptions, and a personal interpretation of how things should be. All of these things produce and allow you to keep emotions alive, find and recruit others around you with similar viewpoints, and in many cases influence future responses you may have. Personal replay of world events or entertainment that has evoked an emotional response is shared with co-workers, family friends and total strangers. This allows the replay to foster, evolve and mold your opinions and personal beliefs.

Notice we include others before our final conclusions are reached. Even if you had a preconceived opinion, you may not "own" this until others have shared their opinion. Our personal lives are becoming so open today. When we are in emotional conflict, we surround ourselves with similar thinkers to acquire clarity and a course of action to take. We demand validation for choices we've already made, and for emotional outbursts we've experienced. Some of the above you may feel is an inaccurate description of yourself, but I know you know these people and share these traits. To some degree, we all participate in this condition, and the new generation now entering adulthood are masters. But this is because we trained them, and fostered this evolution within today's society and in ourselves.

The outcome is a continual state of drama and emotion. It's an addiction that prevents us from living our lives versus watching lives; having discussions versus judging others; encouraging us to look for what's wrong versus what's right; and seeing only black and white when we should be embracing the grey. We feel powerless in our lives and in world events, and attribute all self-worth to being experts on others and how things should be accomplished.

Being an authority on everyone else allows us to feed our egos and release "feel good" hormones that give us the boost necessary to combat our own stress hormones. Stress is a killer and it produces hormones that wear out our bodies and make us susceptible to disease, and in society today there is an endless supply of stimuli for it. The use of and participation in drama is only a quick fix to the drama addict, but luckily, like with any addiction, we have the power to choose and change it.

Being a drama junkie is not only a bad habit, but a taught behavior. Drama may not be completely removed from our daily existence; we are natural-born story-tellers and need human connection. Even so, it is possible to remove yourself from riding the daily drama bus and give yourself the control to start living your life again with the tools to steer your own vehicle of self- management. You've always had this ability and power, and now you will have the owner manual.

"If you create your own storm, don't get angry if you get stuck in the rain."

~C. Tang~

2 REMOVING TRIGGERS

"Letting go" is one of the most challenging parts of this process for many. We spend so much time, energy and emotional resources on catastrophizing. Catastrophizing is an irrational or exaggerated thought that something is far worse than the reality. It can manifest through fearing the worst, or anticipating all the things that could go wrong. This is usually accompanied by a lack of self-confidence and a feeling that you have no control over your situation.

Removing yourself from this negative cycle may seem impossible, as the perception that this is a trait permanently ingrained has taken hold and convinced you that this is part of your internal make-up. This is not the case. Every situation, every encounter, and every task has an internal running dialog that has been expelled vocally over and over again until the dialog moves to the next dilemma. The anxieties that form from this destructive habit are harmful, intrude on the lives of those around you, and prevent self-improvement. It prevents a person from seeing other viewpoints, keeping them in a constant state of right and wrong, good or bad.

Imagine the world with the sun illuminating the planet. Only the side closest to the sun is lit and the opposite side is in complete darkness. What about all the places in the world now experiencing dawn and dusk? They are not in a state of light or darkness. The same can be said for your thoughts of right and wrong. The world is so much bigger and has more to offer when we are able to see the grey. If you can identify with this, are ready to admit this is a cycle you've been participating in, and are willing to be open to change, you can be deprogrammed.

Be aware, though, of others around you who are also participating in this cycle. Imagine your emotional stability is in an internal bank vault. With every positive and uplifting thought or emotion your bank receives a deposit, and with every exposure to negativity your bank receives a withdrawal. Now if you are surrounded by people who are continuously demanding your participation in their negative cycle, your emotional stability will quickly become depleted and you will be left overdrawn and unable give anything to others, never mind to yourself. Many of you are already here. Accept this deposit into your emotional bank: You deserve to be happy, powerful and fulfilled.

There is always a running dialog playing inside your head. You'll ask questions, ponder ideas, make statements and even humor yourself. This has been called "mind chatter," "self dialog," and "inner talk," but we will use the term "self-talk." "Self-talk" is the way we internally talk to ourselves continuously, even when we are listening to others and speaking ourselves. Through this continual inner narration we contemplate, learn, judge, assume, form ideas, reflect and produce emotions. Have you ever heard the saying "you can't stop the grapevine"? Well our self-talk is our own personal grapevine. We can't stop it, but we can input and change what the grapevine talks about.

Activity A: Be aware and take note of the self-talk you're participating in. How often are you being critical of yourself? How often are you being judgmental of others and their actions? You will be surprised how often this happens (watching the news, following social media, walking through the mall, driving your car, at work and even with your partners and/or children)

Here are some examples of possible self-talk tracks:

- OMG, who wears that?
- Just look at her hair!
- If those were my kids, I'd...
- I love that _____ - on someone else.
- I wish I was...
- How dare they...
- I can't believe they...

Etc...

Bus Stop

Take a few days or a week to fully participate in Activity A.

Suggested activity: Write nightly journal entries on your day. Reflect on what thoughts you had about other people, situations and events. Don't judge your self-talk, simply acknowledge it and observe how many times this dialog runs and what it is saying.

Activity B: Start the reconditioning of self-talk by first recognizing the thought, and then giving yourself an alternative thought.

Here are some examples of possible "self-talk," and how we can consciously stop ourselves by inputting a new thought.

- Hear...Why doesn't she just leave him? Input...I might not know the whole story, I wish her well.
- Hear...What a stupid driver, he shouldn't have a license. Input...I've done that too, it's so embarrassing.
- Hear...How hard is it really to make a workable schedule for me? Input...I bet it is hard to manage so many people.
- Hear...If that was my kid, I'd stop that quickly. Input...Parenting is hard.
- Hear...He doesn't deserve that promotion. Input...Good for him, I'm sure he'll do a great job.
- Hear...Must be nice to have Daddy's money. Input...What a nice car (insert item).

Life, situations and people are not black and white. There is always another viewpoint. You cannot predict outcomes or be certain of anything. Question yourself – why are you thinking that? Does it make you feel better? Who says it's wrong? Are you better at controlling your life choices than anyone else?

This activity will be eye-opening. The sheer number of times we claim superiority over others will shock you. Adding an alternative viewpoint to your self-talk can be as habit-forming as the original thought. You've been conditioned over years and this will take time and practice to overcome, or at least correct quickly. While doing this, resist judging yourself. You may be so taken aback by what you've been saying and the opinions you've been forming that you end up turning on yourself with feelings of shallowness, shame and regret. Focusing on self-damnation is counterproductive. You've only done what you've been taught. Choose instead to take back control with new taught behaviors.

So what is a trigger? Triggers are outside influences that affect your emotional state. A positive emotion can be triggered by a show of appreciation, a thank you, a movie, a hug, a happy memory, or anything that makes you feel special. A negative trigger would be something that produces a response of anger, resentment, jealously, or disappointment. It could be caused by an unpleasant memory, or anything that produces stress: an abuse video online, a political debate, a lottery winner, a message from a friend who's hurting, people protesting, beautiful places you've never been, destructive world events, lifestyle reality shows and posts on social media.

Many people in literary circles will tell you to remove all negative triggers and surround yourself with only a positive environment. Though adopting a "positivity only" lifestyle is a wonderful idea in theory, it's not very realistic. In my daily life, even after removing social media, the news and negative people, I am still in contact with life events, coworkers, family drama and people I may not be able to avoid. There will always be the person or situation that seems to push your buttons, no matter how hard you try to rise above.

Can't determining what a negative or harmful influence is be a judgment in itself? Yes – but if we agree life and people are not black and white, then the idea of what is right or wrong, good or bad, becomes blurred. The influences around us may or may not be harmful, and this is something we must each determine for ourselves. But how?

From your observation and analysis of the self-talk activity, you can accurately determine what provokes an emotional response. What elements are you exposed to that encourage you to become judgmental and critical of others? Until you are able to take control of your negative self-talk, you may choose to temporarily remove elements and/or people from your daily life.

Some examples:

- You're watching the news and your self-talk prejudges what is right and wrong
- Your favorite reality show provokes judgmental thoughts, based on another person's appearance or abilities
- Your favorite sports team evokes a desire to inflict pain and destruction on players of the opposing team
- Your social media feed is a flurry of superior opinions, daily dramas and unjust events, leaving you either depressed or negativity simulated (feeling an urge to participate)
- Your conversations with your best friend are a constant re-enactment of other people's lives, and your combined opinions take on a self-righteous tone
- Your family member calls or visits and your self-esteem feels shattered. This may be because they have compared you to others, or due to the pressure you put on yourself to be positively perceived

In all of these examples, you can choose to temporarily remove the related triggers from your daily life. Turn off the TV, Facebook and Twitter. Screen your calls, and take a sabbatical from certain people.

Recently I had to do my own self check on social media. My friend Lydia's marriage has been torn from her. She found out she's pregnant, but the baby daddy is not committed to being a father. Lydia is bitter with her husband for ending the marriage, angry at herself for getting pregnant and frustrated with the baby daddy for his distance. She channels her anger and frustration onto social media. Other drama junkies weigh in and some of these women can be brutal with their attacks. Friends and family race to the defense and more posts of retaliation soon follow.

The baby is born, but the drama addiction is still present. Amongst the newborn photos come the posts of daily baby-dad updates, relationship crisis, and maternal hardship. Now granted Lydia is quite young and has had an enormous amount of responsibility thrust upon her in a very short time. I really like her, feel for her situation, and understand where the emotions have come from. However, these posts, the language, the anger, and the drama that ensues are now affecting my wellbeing and I have a choice to make.

I un-followed her. Now, I could have also un-friended her, but I do wish her the best, like her as a person and hope this is only a temporary action for a temporary behavior. I told her mother to keep me in the loop and to keep posting pictures of the baby. It's not up to me to judge Lydia, her discussions or what is healthy for her, but I can decide and take action on this for myself.

Resist telling yourself this is a permanent commitment. Once your self-talk is open to all possibilities, outcomes, diversity, and viewpoints, the value you placed on these triggers will change. Not because you were told to change (though we will talk about reintegration later), but because you have grown to a different place and no longer feel the need to supply your ego with drama.

"Most powerful is he who has himself in his own power."

~Seneca~

Bus Stop

Give yourself a few days or a week to fully participate in Activity B.

Suggested activity: Review your journal from the last Bus Stop and continue to journal triggering events. Before you continue, you can now decide what activities to temporarily remove from your life.

3 EMOTIONAL DETACHMENT

To be able to focus on solutions versus problems, you need the ability to remove yourself from emotional baggage and thus expand your options. Emotional reactions to situations do not allow you to fully examine the options you have, nor do they give you the power to take control. They evoke more negative emotions that prevent you from moving forward. Feelings like, "of course this would happen," "every time," "I can't," "what if," and "always." Because the situation causes an emotional response, many times we'll reflect back with worry, regret, fear, assumptions, predictions, blame, or frustration. Did you know that the definition of frustration is "the prevention of progress, success, or fulfillment of something"?

After we react to a situation, we'll often surround ourselves with other people who validate our thoughts or share similar opinions. Recently I was at a workshop where an example was used that I found fitting to this type of situation.

An employee (who we'll call Betty) is told they must attend a work function. Betty does not want to attend and feels forced into the situation, which starts the framework for an emotional response. Her self-talk is telling her that the event will be boring, stupid, and unproductive, and she asks herself, "Why do I always get dragged out to these affairs?"

At the party she walks in with a plastered smile, but is not in the mood to mingle, nor will she allow her mindset to change. She makes her way to a corner food table and checks out the selection, arranging herself a plate. Soon others also make their way to this table and a small group forms. Eventually they connect and start talking about how the event is stupid, boring and a complete waste of time, each participant validating and inflating the others' viewpoint.

Was this a fair representation of the function? Or were there people who came open to the event with the intention of having a good time, making it fun, and enjoying the evening? Yes, there were. These people did enjoy the evening, found it a good use of their time, and would gladly attend again. As attendance was mandatory and none of the employees were there by choice, it was a matter of looking at the options they had available and choosing their attitude and reaction to the event before attending.

The people who enjoy an event don't usually notice those in the "corner of doom," as it isn't part of the world they are choosing to live in at that moment. To bring control back into your life and objectively make choices, you need to first be able to manage those emotional moments by course-correcting your self-talk and detaching yourself from the situation, so you can better examine your options and move forward.

Emotionally detaching yourself does not mean you deny yourself the ability to experience emotions. This is part of human nature and very specific to each individual person; different people will experience a different degree of emotion when experiencing the same situation. When a negative emotion is triggered, give yourself permission to feel it. Then work on detaching yourself from the feeling.

Some tips:

- Listen to yourself and keep practicing your self-talk tracking
- Go for a walk, hit the gym, or lift weights
- Cook, clean, landscape, paint, or start a new craft
- Look for things in your life to feel grateful for. Call them out and say "thank you" (the sun, a flower, a song, family, your pet, etc...)
- My favorite example is meditation, as it relaxes and refocuses the brain

Know at these times, though, that taking action or making decisions needs to be delayed until you can move past the emotion. Also remember that it's all temporary – the good and the bad. Avoid posting on social media (Facebook, Twitter, etc…), calling your friend to reflect on it, or enlightening your co-workers, as this will only feed the negative emotion and create more drama.

Though this may sound simple, to a drama junkie this withdrawal stage may be incredibly difficult. The emotion itself is not bad; it is the reaction to the emotion (internally and externally) that we want to change. I would also recommend avoiding hard substances during this transition period. Use of these substances can heighten the existing emotions, and possibly bring other destructive thoughts to surface (resentment, depression, etc…).

"The self is not something ready-made, but something in continuous formation through choice of action."

~John Dewey~

Be wary of feeling that you've mastered this step, or that it's safe to take shortcuts, as detachment is a lifelong process that will never be fully mastered. Let's look at an example of someone who feels they have mastered this step by turning things over to Karma. What is Karma? Karma is a principle of cause and effect, where the intent and actions of an individual will determine future happiness or suffering. Basically it's a law that states if you do good, good things will happen to you. However on the flipside if you had negative actions or intent, then the future will hold some of the same for you. Now that we have established what Karma is, let's talk about Cyndy who thinks she can detach from her emotions by turning everything undesirable that happens in her life over to Karma.

Cyndy thinks she can detach from her emotions by turning everything undesirable in her life over to karma. She has come to the point of accepting the reality that she has no control over the outcome of certain situations and events. Her idea of detachment is that, if she feels wronged by another person, she will simply tell karma to "get them," and then tell others how she detached... "But they'll get theirs."

In one particular situation, she has even told the person who had wronged her that "karma is coming for you." I'm afraid the lesson here has been lost. The negative emotion has still been allowed to fester, the dramatization is still running rampant, and Cyndy is feeling that her belief in karma has not only given her power over another person, but that the universe will deliver justice on her behalf.

One of my favorite quotes is, *"How people treat you is their karma; how you react is yours" ~Wayne Dyer ~* and Cyndy (like all of us) has not reacted well. She thought she had mastered detachment, but the reality isn't so simple. When we are ready to remove the power we give to others to control our actions, behaviors' and emotions, then we can react without ill-will, damning thoughts or superiority. Their actions belong to them. Your thoughts and actions belong to you. I truly do believe in karma, not as a way to deal out justice, but as a philosophy of peace and love which starts inside you. In this new emotional place, there is no need for "pay-back."

Emotional detachment takes continuous practice. You might see a car accident on your way to work. When you arrive at work, you could find a co-worker being abusive, or have an overwhelming workload on a deadline. At the end of the day, you might come home to a teenager's fit and the house destroyed, find your partner is going out once again, or find someone has been talking about you behind your back. Over the course of months or years, these daily situations will start affecting your mental health if emotion overtakes logic with every response. It's no wonder instances of mental illness have sky-rocketed in North America. To be able to detach effectively, you need to address each situation individually as it occurs.

Bus Stop

Take a few minutes and process some past situations.

- Were you being affected emotionally?
- Might you have reacted differently if you weren't emotionally compromised?

Take a mental break here to keep your thoughts in check.

OK....Ready?

Good!

Let's go and move forward.

When we delve into choices, you can take back control of your path, but trying to address a lifetime of events all at once will add to anyone's stress levels. This is about taking those baby steps, looking at each situation individually and detaching from it. Forgive yourself and give yourself permission to falter and make mistakes, all while forming solid coping habits that can be used in your daily life. Our purpose here is to take back the power in our lives one emotion at a time. There will always be an event that feels overwhelming and will take time and steps to process before reacting, but they will become fewer and you will have the skills and confidence to see them through.

Once you feel that you can look objectively at your situations, then you can start the process of really looking at what your options are. What are the potential outcomes, and which choice will provide the best plan moving forward? At this point, you may also find that you want to solicit the opinion of an outside source (family, a friend, your therapist, etc.). Ensure that this person is someone you trust to be objective and who will not feed or over-dramatize the situation. You need a sounding board only to explore options or to help redefine the situation from a different viewpoint and explore potential outcomes. Avoid taking on a confidant who wants to give you solutions, fix the situation, or fix you. It is important for you to take the control back as we move forward. You need to believe in your own ability to be a decision-maker, and allow others around you to do the same.

"True detachment isn't a separation from life, but the absolute freedom within your mind to explore life."

~Ron W. Rathbun~

4 POWER OF CHOICE

Now that you have the ability to remove the emotional barriers, you are ready to explore choices. Every situation has multiple options to choose from. Not every choice is on the consideration board, but all, even the ones you would never choose, are available. As an example, let's look back at our employee, Betty; what were her choices once she was told of the mandatory event she had to attend?

- Go and have a horrible time
- Go and pretend to enjoy it
- Go but resent having to
- Go and make the best of it
- Go with the intention of building relationships
- Go and have a great time
- Don't go and file a complaint
- Don't go and risk her job
- Don't go and look for other work
- Don't go and quit

The choices are limitless. Some may not be options you feel are worth considering, and each choice produces a different set of potential outcomes.

Information gathering is an important part of decision-making. Consider the following example:

An employer sits down with an employee and presents the dreaded documentation. The employee has been written-up due to some information that has been brought to the employer, but because it was from only one viewpoint, the situation is not entirely accurate. Since the employer made the choice to do the documentation without investigating all sides, the employee is now defensive and angry. Upon hearing another side to the situation, the employer now feels the documentation is inaccurate, but the damage has already been done.

Many times we make poor choices because we react to the situation before we gather all the necessary information. There is no time-limit allotted to you, no deadline you need to follow; you do need to act, but you need to first give yourself time to gather information and process it before moving forward.

Purchasing a vehicle can be a very difficult choice for many people. Would it be better to stop in at a dealership, see a suitable model, talk to the salesman, get swept away in desire and make a purchase that day? Or would it be wise to determine your wants and needs, research a variety of options, and then take all of that information to the desired dealership and talk to that salesman? It still might not be the best choice, but you made it without being driven by emotion and with confidence in the information you gathered.

This may seem a pretty easy idea to implement, but this is the area in which many people find their downfall or revert to past behaviors. Sometimes this can be due to missing information, ill-considered choices, or unforeseen outcomes, but many times it's due to a mental barrier like resentment or over-thinking.

Resentment comes from not being able to make your own choices due to another's person's decision. As an example, I recently talked to a lady regarding her ex-husband of over 20 years. She was very angry and bitter, as the marriage ended due to no choice of hers. After the separation, she fell into many destructive relationships, and though she worked to support the family, she began drinking which severely damaged her finances and personal ties.

Years later, she overcame the drinking, rebuilt her career and worked on her relationship with her children. She was financially secure, and her relationships had been mended while she rebuilt herself. But even through all her obstacles and personal growth, she was still incredibly angry. When talking with this woman, I asked her why she was still so upset with her previous husband – after all, it had been 20 years.

Her answer was that she was angry because her ex was in a much more secure place in his life than she was. She didn't feel it was fair that she had been dealt struggles and hardships that prevented the same outcome for her. Though she was able to recover and take control of her life again, she still couldn't find a place without drama, because her ex was still her trigger.

Now that this barrier had been identified, we looked at each life path separately. Since her ex didn't have the same anger barrier, he was able to make different choices, like a career, savings and investments. We talked at length about her choices, his choices and where both of them were today. There were two main points to the conversation: 1) The choices each person made in their separate lives, and how those decisions had brought them to two very different places, and 2) Which life would she prefer to have – not in bits and pieces, but in its entirety?

Ultimately, she picked her own life, as she really valued her relationships with her children and genuinely liked the person she had become. I then asked her, if her choices brought her to today and his choices did the same, why was she so full of resentment? The reason she gave was that she didn't *want* any of the choices she'd had to make. She wanted the married life with the little white picket fence, and because he ended the marriage, she no longer had that choice.

Because this resentment had never been addressed, it created a cascade of destructive choices. Had acceptance been reached all those years ago, then things might have played out very differently. After our talk, she went to seek professional help, and now is happier than she's ever been. Today she is making choices that are healthier for her and has found a place of forgiveness, not just for not just for Mr. X, but also for herself.

Now let's look a reverse situation. Jenny is in a long-term relationship, but is left feeling unsatisfied. Though she's contemplating leaving the relationship, she still cares deeply for her boyfriend and doesn't want to lose him from her life or cause him any pain. He is very committed to her, and wishes to work things out even though he knows they have problems.

She could break up with him and walk away; recommit and work towards finding the happiness she desires within the relationship; or she could stay in limbo with him, hoping for resolution. Jenny is familiar both with making choices, and also with what it's like being on the receiving end of someone else's decision, so she hesitates.

Taking time to process and weigh out all your options and their effects is very healthy, up to a point. First, there may be numerous potential outcomes to each choice, which she'd have no control over. Second, there is another person's emotional well-being at stake – a person she cares about – and remaining in a state of limbo that could hurt him further down the road is selfish. Jenny doesn't want to decide, as she's unsure which the correct course of action is.

One of the truths about life is that every action has a reaction, or many possible reactions, and some outcomes of choices we make redirect our path into unknown territory. Knowing this isn't helping Jenny make her choice, and the real problem is that, once the choice is made, she must commit to that path, and the outcome may not be one she desires. As an example: she would have already made the choice to part ways if he would be guaranteed to stay in her life as a friend. But in reality, once they part, whether or not he stays in her life will become his choice and not hers. Knowing this throws her into turmoil. In another example: they separate and 10 years later she looks back only to realize that leaving this relationship had been a mistake, and now he's married with three kids.

Once Jenny makes a decision, she'll be able to move forward, whatever the path. It is true that the magnitude of certain choices will follow us throughout our lives, and not all are the good or right choices we hoped for. Even so, they do need to be made, and with each leap of faith we must accept the outcome, or risk the emotional baggage of regret or wondering. Commit to your path, or beware... Your choice just might get made for you.

The feeling of power and control comes from the ability to choose. In the termination of a relationship, there is in most cases one person who is the dumper and one the dumped. The dumper has the knowledge that the relationship will no longer continue. The person who is dumped moves into a state of grieving, including shock or disbelief, denial, bargaining, guilt, anger, depression, and acceptance/hope. The loss in many cases interrupts their family, social networks, professional productivity, and their personal life.

The "dumped" must now move forward and make new life choices, even though the choice to be at this crossroad was thrust upon them. They feel out of control, helpless and powerless. The "dumper" went through their own personal emotional stages, including dread, anticipation, guilt, and indecision right up to the point of the confrontation. Soon after, these emotions are met with relief. Not that the feelings prior have been replaced, but empowerment has been given to this person through taking control, making a choice, and following through with the decision. This act gave him/her the power to take control of their future. This does not mean that you should quickly end a relationship before the choice of doing so is taken away from you. Understand that both parties have suffered, both are raw, scared and vulnerable, but it's a perfect example of how the power of choice can empower us, and how a loss of this same power will leave us feeling helpless and out of control.

A relationship is only one example of a situation affecting you and your life direction. Other examples include the loss of a job or promotion, a personal rejection, the loss of a home, financial restrictions, etc… But this isn't about blame. The circumstances you are facing are usually impacted by a sequence of events that you played a part in. This is about being able to move forward from an impasse where you feel you have been placed.

Taking charge is about looking objectively at your available choices, not focusing on or investing emotion into a choice that has been removed by someone else. When you feel powerless and helpless, this is usually a warning beacon that your life or your situation is moving in a certain direction without your say-so or approval. It is not realistic to think that everything is completely within your control, or that life will unfold as you desire. There is, however, a way to regain empowerment.

First, you must accept the impasse or situation you are in. Take the time to think about it, analyze, grieve, etc… Do you have any choices that change the path you are walking down right now? YES! You have many choices that will impact your future. Can you change the fact that you are here at this impasse? NO! Maybe you would have changed the past, maybe not…but the fact remains that it happened, and it may not have been by your choice. Knowing this and accepting where you are will allow you to look ahead and let go of what brought you to this place. From a place of acceptance, you can then make choices moving ahead that will empower you. Trying to move forward with the baggage of resentment only weighs you down and prevents you from seeing all your options clearly.

Over thinking is another barrier that will prevent you from either making a choice, or committing to a made choice. This comes from fear, in most cases. A fear of making a mistake, a fear of making the wrong choice, or a fear of being concerned with what others may think of you. Consider the example below:

A couple discovers they have only 4 years left on their mortgage, but the home is in need of renovations. They look at all their options and decide on the course of action to take. The next day, the husband reconsiders the choice, afraid that years later this might turn out to be a mistake. He talks to others to solicit advice, and changes his mind yet again. He then turns to the internet for advice, and family weighs in. Finally, the husband is so confused that a state of limbo begins. Had the original choice been made and done, years of stress and uncompleted projects might not have followed.

Getting information and doing research before making a large decision is a great idea, but eventually a choice does need to be made and committed to. Again, you need to believe that you can make decisions, but also give yourself permission to make the wrong ones. Remove yourself from the judgment of others and what they perceive as being right and wrong. Since humans are not black and white we can take solace in the grey. There is no need to re-evaluate and get caught in a revolving door of indecision. You'll become more confident with each positive outcome, while learning and growing with each mistake. It's a win-win.

"It's choice - not chance - that determines your destiny."

~Jean Nidetch~

5 MAKING THE CHOICE

If making a choice without the input or approval of others is new to you, then you may need a guide:

- Take stock of the situation
- Stop and do a personal inventory
    - Are you emotionally detached?
    - Do you have all the necessary information?
    - Are you being influenced by external forces?
- What are all the options available to you, (even the ones you wouldn't consider)?
- What are all the possible outcomes to each choice? (If this is new to you, a pen and paper may be required)
- Remove from your list the choices that are not an option
- Look at the remaining choices
- Check that all possible outcomes have been considered
- Don't get caught up in emotions (e.g. wishing a choice was there that isn't)
- Stay rational, objective and clear-headed… NOW CHOOSE

Once you have made your decision, it's done. Commit to the actions needed and make them happen. If this turns out to be a mistake, that's okay, you gave yourself permission and you'll learn from it and move forward. Your mind can be at peace.

When a choice turns out to be a mistake, the key is to look at why. Was there a different choice that hadn't been considered? Was there necessary information you didn't have? Was there an unexpected outcome? Making mistakes is fantastic for learning about yourself and other people, and for absorbing lessons that will impact future decisions.

"True wisdom comes to each of us when we realize how little we understand about life, ourselves, and the world around us."

~Socrates~

Becky was in a relationship that she felt might need to be terminated. We sat down and wrote out all the reasons the relationship was a good match that added value to her life. Then we wrote down all the reasons the relationship was not working. The lists were pretty equal. Becky then was asked what failings from the second list she could live with – after all, nobody is perfect. There were about five items remaining. Then we wrote out her choices.

She wrote that she could…

- stay in the relationship and be happy, even while knowing these issues were there
- stay and the relationship and be silently unhappy
- stay in the relationship and bitch, whine and moan (which she had been doing)
- give an ultimatum for change
- tell him how she's feeling
- terminate the relationship and move on
- decide not to make a decision YET

We then removed any choices that were not considerations for her. She was left with…

- giving an ultimatum
- talking to him about how she's feeling
- terminating the relationship and moving on

Now what could be the outcomes?

- Giving an ultimatum (confrontation, threats, follow-through of threats, rejection, defensiveness, frustration, the end of the relationship, refusal, receiving critical feedback, etc…)
- Talking to him about how she's feeling (confrontation, defensiveness, indifference, compliance, potential solutions, receiving critical feedback, compromise, the relationship ends, etc…)
- Terminating the relationship and moving on (confrontation, guilt, sorrow, elation, regret, grief, happiness, insecurity, etc...)

Becky made a choice and decided to talk to her partner about how she was feeling. I connected with her after they had talked. She felt content about her choice, and found it had removed the feelings of helplessness. I don't know what the details of their talk were, but I am told they both shared what each of them did to contribute to the relationship barriers, and that they came to a compromise of what would work for them both.

About a month later, he broke it off and the relationship ended. He expressed that, after their talk, the relationship required more than he was willing to give. Becky was upset, but bounced back quickly as she had been ready to end things a month earlier. Did she make a mistake, or pick the wrong choice? It could have been over a month earlier and on her terms. When I asked, she said she felt the satisfaction of knowing she had given it every chance to succeed and won't have to wonder if things might have turned out differently with an alternative choice.

On a side note regarding ultimatums – whether in a relationship, a conversation at work, or with your children, friends, etc... – ensure this is not out of an emotional impulse. In that situation, you may end up getting your wish and moving on, but in most cases you need to be willing to act upon that threat, or face having the choice thrust upon you. By not acting on the threat given, your credibility for all future conversations will be questioned. Having your ultimatum put upon you may put you in a position you really didn't want to be in, and now many of your choices moving forward have been removed. If you really have an ultimatum that will be the deciding factor in your relationship, ensure you are willing to follow through with it.

"The more I learn, the less I realize I know."

~Socrates~

Sometimes a mistake we have made is crystal clear. I shouldn't have made the choice in my teenage years to start smoking. I don't need to spell out the health risks, the loss of money, or the social repercussions to anyone today. When there is a realization of error, it is an opportunity to stop, reflect and start the process again, leading into a new set of choices and a new series of outcomes. Each time you make a mistake, you'll get better at the choice-making process. You'll ultimately be more confident with your choices and faster at going through the whole process.

There will be times when you feel unable to make a choice. If you are having trouble deciding, or feel unwilling to deal with a known outcome, you may choose not to make a choice at this time. This is also in your power.

Lily is in a long-term marriage with children. Her husband spends all their money, goes out partying, and leaves all child-rearing and household duties to Lily. Lily is frustrated with her work-load, worried about finances, and feels unappreciated and very alone. She has already gone through the process outlined above, and decided to talk to her husband about how she feels.

She requested they go to talk to someone together and work on their marriage. This discussion didn't go over very well, and an agreement or compromise was never reached. This situation isn't about who's right or wrong; as we're not in their home, we don't know how they communicate, what their history is, or what past conversations have taken place. We do know that Lily is at a place where she needs to make a choice going forward. She decided that since Christmas was coming, she would wait until January to re-examine her situation. This was her choice.

If you choose to delay making a decision, there are two known factors. Either you will have to consider your choices again at a later date and make a decision then, OR a new choice will present itself that wasn't possible before. In any case, Lily will have to make a choice, and she may choose to stay and live her life as it has been in the past, or she may make a change, but it's her choice.

Regardless of the action you take, you made the choice. Even delaying a decision is a choice. But once a choice has been made, you are no longer a victim to your situation. You choose it. You have the power, and you will react differently to a situation when you're choosing to be there versus feeling like you're a hostage to your circumstances.

Right now, this process is taking effort, thought and preparation: removing those outside sources and emotional attachments; the time and energy put into evaluating; the process of thinking through choices and outcomes; as well as a commitment to a choice and a willingness to make mistakes. Eventually though, like any taught behavior, all of this will become habit forming, like behavioral muscle memory. It will be a repeatable routine that is a part of the subconscious mind, and will only require deeper attention during major or life-changing events.

"The strongest principle of growth lies in human choice."

~George Eliot~

6 NEUTRALIZE DRAMA

Facebook now has a new "live" feature which is fast becoming the trend. Franka runs a Facebook group and has been doing regular lives for her group, friends and family. A virtual passerby sees her live feed and is compelled to leave a less than positive comment – in fact it was downright nasty.

Franka sees this comment, and now has some choices to make. Does she reply defensively, get depressed and quit, do a second "live" in retaliation, ignore the comment, delete the comment, or rally up some supporters? I couldn't have been prouder of what she did. She replied to the comment, thanking him for watching and wishing him well. On her next "live," she addressed the comment to say only that she had used it to self-reflect and grow. The result is…nothing. No drama ensues, no posse of supporters goes on the war path, and no attack is launched.

Franka's response may not be the one you would have chosen for yourself, but for Franka it felt right. She took the time to detach, weighed out her choices and the potential consequences/outcomes, and then made the right choice for her.

You are now in control of your life and the direction you take it in. The drama bus doesn't stop for you, nor do you pay its fare. You might now be at a place where you miss some of those contacts who rode the bus with you regularly, or some past entertainment you used to enjoy. You can make these choices and decide who you want to associate with, and what you want to do in your leisure-time.

Do take caution and maintain continual self-checks. It is easier to revert to past habits than to maintain a new one. If you find yourself back on the drama bus, get off at the next stop and monitor your self-talk and your emotions. Some people may no longer be compatible with you, now that you've grown into a self-aware being. Some entertainment may no longer hold value for you, and you can allow it to dissolve into your past.

This journey was to help you regain your power. This power comes from a greater understanding of yourself and a greater respect for the ability to take back some control in your life. I truly believe this will only be a step in your journey, as a new world of self-empowered discovery awaits you.

"To find yourself, think for yourself."

~Socrates~

PARK THE DRIVER

As we slow to a stop I wanted to take a moment to conclude these thoughts. As outlined in this text, there is a huge amount of empowerment in choice. Now that you can freely make your own choices, you must also be confident in your ability to step out in front of the bus and survive (metaphorically of course).

When I was at a place of publishing this guide, I was doing exactly this. I had to look at the emotions of fear, comparison and potential judgment. As this moment my thoughts are only on my computer, and there is no real danger. It's all in my head. Now I'm writing this from a place of vulnerability, as most authors of any self help books appear confident and all knowing. Not the case. We write what we know.

I monitored my words both inside and out, adjust their direction and contemplated my choices and the outcomes. Here was the conclusion.... I needed to go to print and share this with the world! Though I may have undesired reviews or have the content questioned, I believe in the foundation of self empowerment provided here. I personally live this daily and have assisted hundreds more to do the same.

If this content helps or touches even one person than I am successful. More importantly, I will have the pride in the knowledge that I took this to completion, overcame a fear; and though I am in front of the bus...I will survive and bloom! The bus is only an illusion, and it's my choice to get run over, get on, or simply wave it by.

I hope you too will stop the drama bus and get off, with the feeling that you now have the power to overcome any obstacle ... after all it's all in your head as it was in mine.

"Stop acting so small. You are the universe in ecstatic motion"

~Rumi~

TRANSPORT NEW PASSENGERS

The Generation Gap

Each generation has their own trends and traits that were passed down from the previous generation, and is affected by different values, attitudes, and interests. Each generation experiences differences in the current technology and witnessed different historical events. Understanding the differences between generations helps bring to light why parenting has changed from the time when we were parented, and why some techniques are no longer effective. This can help a parent better relate to and communicate with their offspring. Some past generations were motivated by status and title, some wanted to change the world, and others were about balance.

For now, let's just discuss those born after the 80's: the Millennial Generation, Generation Why, Ego Boomers, or Generation Me. This generation has been getting a bad rap in social media lately, but coming from someone who works closely with these people and calls many of them friends, I'd like to clear a few things up.

This generation is the one that has mastered multitasking, especially when it concerns technology, and is made up of team-players. They are public with all their life events, networking encompasses their daily lives, and their social network is always close at hand. This continuous daily conversation is normal to them, and a vital part of daily life. They need to always know what they are doing right and what they are doing wrong, and like to give their own opinions to others. Silence is an indicator to this generation that they aren't being noticed, or that they're not important.

They are civic minded, have strong social opinions, and readily reject what society has determined to be the norm. Millennials need to feel that they are a part of the establishment, and like to know they are offering an immediate contribution, even if just in a small way.

As these individuals have parents, are becoming parents, and are either in or entering the workplace, I wanted to add these extra chapters.

1 PARENT MANUAL

The most important role you have as a parent is ensuring and encouraging the birth of an independent adult. Unfortunately, millennials have been told they are entitled to everything, and consequently they believe it. This creates narcissism as normal, accepted behavior, and gives parents, employers, and educators a run for their money.

If you are appalled right now and disagree, either because you are a millennial raising children, or because you're saying as the parent of a millennial, "My child was NOT raised this way," this may well be true. But it is equally true that their friends, classmates, coworkers, social networking contacts, and the media are facilitating this thought process. We see the evidence with parents attacking the educational system and placing fault on the educator for their child's lack of achievement.

As children enter their teens, an interest in material gain accompanied by behavioral outbursts is justified. As young adults, parents come to job interviews, follow-up with employers who dare enforce policy, and encourage the neglecting of commitments in favor of family events. Ultimately, this group of public, self-absorbed drama junkies are the drivers of the drama bus, but they lack the coping skills necessary for independent decision-making to guide them into adulthood. If at this point you're offended, keep reading. I'm in your corner and have raised a child born after the 80's.

From a very young age, the concepts outlined in this chapter can be utilized. As a toddler, the only real drama is that of the self and the reactions expressed by others. If a child gets a reaction to a situation, then this is a taught behavior he or she is learning. As a parent, we are either told to or learn to ignore undesirable behaviors from our child, in order to prevent a repeat performance brought about by the reaction received.

Parents who have mastered this can attest to the positive results. This is a prime example of parental emotional detachment. The parent may be shocked, amused, or embarrassed, but regardless of the emotion, none of it is shown or expressed to the child. Now take this strategy into the world of choice. The younger the child, the more simplified the choices will be. As an example:

Child: "I want ________."

Parent: "No honey, not today."

In response, the child has an emotional fit of frustration, possibly with bargaining, yelling, and arguing.

If this happens to you, don't react. This is one of those unwanted behaviors that shouldn't be fed into, even if the child adds a personal attack, like "I hate you." Don't take it personally, instead give them a choice.

Parent: "You can keep getting upset about this and ______consequence______ or we can carry on having a good day."

The choice given could be one of multiple things, like a timeout or leaving the store. Now let them make the choice. You are not only bringing peace to a hectic household, you are also empowering your child with the life lesson of choice.

The most important piece of this strategy is following through. When a choice is presented with a consequence, you must follow-through once the choice is made. First and foremost, you must remain emotionally detached at the time the choice is presented, and again if follow-through is required. By staying calm and detached from any personal emotion, you can clearly present choices you are willing to follow-through with.

Having a consequence presented in anger that could never be followed through with (example: "If you don't smarten up, I will never take you out in public again") will ultimately destroy the lesson of choice. Not being able to follow through teaches the child that they really don't have to decide on this occasion, or on any to follow, because you won't or can't enforce it.

Timeouts as an option can be incredibly valuable to your child, as well as giving you some distance to detach emotionally. Many times this option is a stall until an issue can be addressed more productively. For example:

Parent: "Please brush your teeth before bed."

Child: "No, I don't want to."

Parent: "Well, you can keep arguing or take a timeout to calm down."

At this point, your child might very well throw a fit. Take them to the place used for timeouts. Without a conversation, remove yourself and breathe. Ensure a timeout allows the child ample time to detach from their emotions, as well as you from yours. Once you and your child are both calm, return to your child and continue the conversation.

Parent: "Do you know why you got a time out?"

Child: "Because I wouldn't brush my teeth."

Parent: "No! You got a time out because you chose to keep arguing. Now, are you ready to brush your teeth?"

Hopefully the answer now is "Yes" or you'll be in for a long night. It's important that the behavior is addressed, not the activity. The lesson that must be learned is that:

1) you will follow through

2) the activity is going to happen

3) the situation they are in is their choice, not yours

Use timeouts for yourself, as well, if you feel you are becoming influenced emotionally by your child with feelings of irritation, frustration, or anger. Or maybe you're just feeling emotionally overwhelmed. Tell your child that you need to take a timeout, and arrange how long that timeout will last. Remove yourself from the situation, relax and breathe. Make sure to return to your child at the pre-set time and thank them for allowing you some space. Timeouts are not punishment, they are a necessary and required coping skill for people of all ages, in order for them to refocus and process information. If your child sees their parent taking time for themselves, they won't view being alone as a punishment now or later in life.

Parent: "Could you please put your clothes in the dryer before supper?"

Preteen: "I'll do it later."

Parent: "Later won't work. I need to put a load in."

Preteen: "Then just move my clothes at the same time. It only takes a second."

Parent: "You're right, it does, so you can either do it now, or we will both stay here in the laundry room until this task is completed."

The preteen starts every excuse, from headaches, to blame, to "if supper burns..." The parent calmly waits.

The preteen starts to lose control, getting increasingly angry, and tries to leave the laundry room. Still saying nothing, the parent hugs their child close.

Right now, the preteen just wants their parent out of their space – and possibly out of their life. (Parents really are the worst!) But the parent just keeps hugging them and won't let go, even when there is yelling and kicking and they both fall to the ground.

Now exhausted, the preteen has a good cry in their parent's arms.

Parent: "Are you ready to put your clothes in the dryer?"

Preteen: "Yes."

Now please understand this is a real example (no parents or children were harmed in the making of it), and I'm in no way endorsing physically restraining anyone, but this parent had to follow through on the consequence based on the choice the preteen made. At the time, it was the only quick solution the parent could come up with that would keep her (the parent) calm, and taught the necessary lesson. The clothes were getting done regardless.

It is easy to see how a parent would be too tired to go through all of that, and might just comply with moving the clothes to save themselves the battle. Though the example above probably took over an hour, do you think this preteen argued the next time she was asked to move her clothes to the dryer? Pick and choose your battles, but once you've chosen one, follow through.

Since your primary responsibility as a parent – other than nurturing and safety – is to guide your child into being an independent, fully-functional adult, the pre-teen/teenage years can be the most crucial time to ensure the message of choice is firmly installed.

A mother and teen are going to a yearly Christmas outdoor event. The weather is what you would expect from December – cold. They are meeting up with the rest of the family at 7pm.

Parent: "We have to leave soon, get your coat and boots on"

The teen comes out wearing a thin sweater.

Parent: "You're not wearing that, it's really cold out."

Teen: "I'm not wearing that coat, it make me look like an idiot."

Parent: "Your coat looks fine, but more important, it's warm."

Teen: "I look like a loser."

Parent: "Either you put on your winter coat, or we won't be going."

Teen – "I'm not going if I have to wear that."

The parent picks up the phone, calls the family and informs them they won't be attending. When the family questions why, the parent calmly tells them the teen has chosen to not attend instead of wearing her winter coat.

The family never really understood why a coat would have prevented their attendance, and the parent didn't feel the need to explain the lesson. Many years later, it came out that she was trying to impress a boy… She never met up with the boy that evening, and proceeded to blame her absence on the unfair parent. The teen was angry for a few days, but she got over it and the next time there was an outdoor winter event...she wore her coat.

In today's busy world, these lessons do take time and can be a great inconvenience. Though you, the parent, are making sacrifices, the child might not know this. A child, preteen or teen is pretty self-absorbed right now, and your sacrifice honestly means nothing in comparison to their own discomfort. As a parent, you must accept this and make your own choice to be inconvenienced, or the lesson will be lost.

Middle and high school are full of drama and situations that should give you and your teen ample opportunity to practice. This will be foreign, not only to the teen, but also to the parent. Many parents fall into the trap of "let me be your BFF" or "it's my way or the highway." May I offer an alternative? What if the parent stayed the parent, but was in the role of a consultant?

Here is how that would work. Your teen is given permission to tell you anything, and you will only step in when you feel their safety is in jeopardy. There are some real positive and negative sides to this option. On the plus side, your teen will find you approachable, and it will keep them in a safe mindset, which will open up communications. On the downside, your teen may tell you things you don't want to hear, and test your ability to emotionally detach.

As part of the arrangement, you have to promise yourself that you will stay neutral, calm and honest when questioned. Being honest is crucial for building trust and even if they disagree with your answer, he/she will start to build respect for your viewpoint. When your teen tells you something, you can ask questions and do some activities with "choices," but don't offer your opinion until asked. If you feel your viewpoint is crucial, wait until after the discussion, then ask him/her if it's okay that you give your viewpoint on the situation – either way, respect their answer.

The goal is to open communication, providing you with the ability to guide their choices, create independence, and to advise when called upon. There may be times when your teen just wants to talk it out and doesn't want to be advised, or might choose not to take the advice given. This will be your greatest parenting test, as you watch your child potentially fail or face consequences that could have been avoided if they had only listened.

Teen: "Mom, I want to go to Ben's house after school."

Parent: "Will Ben's parents be home?"

Teen: "His mom will be home later, but probably not until 5 or 6."

Parent: "So you'll be alone for 2-3 hours?"

Teen: "Don't you trust me?"

Parent: "Of course not! I don't trust either of you. You're both a bunch of walking hormones."

Teen: "MOM!!!"

Parent: "I promised you honesty! So let's look at your choices..."

The parent talks with the teen about quite a variety of options. Looking at going, not going, bringing a friend, changing the location, as well as all the possible outcomes of these choices, including getting wrapped up in hormones, STIs and pregnancy. This particular day, the teen chose to bring a friend and they all hung out outside at the pool, but the choice could have gone in any direction. Are you prepared for that? Do you want to know everything your child has to tell you? How much did you tell your parents? This also takes a great deal of time, but if you truly want to build a lasting relationship with your child, you'll make the time and you'll listen to them.

Teen: "Mom, I have a photo-shoot!"

Parent: "A what? And with who?"

The teen takes the parent online to where she had entered to be a model for wedding photographer who was expanding to the graduation audience. (Without asking, I might add.)

Parent: "This does look interesting, and we will look at this, but before we do...can I ask you a question?"

Teen: "Okay."

Parent: "Remember our agreement that I would interfere when I felt your safety was in jeopardy?"

Teen: "Yes, but…"

Parent: "What I am talking about is you submitting your photos online without talking to me about it first. I feel like this sort of behavior is dangerous, and you will not do that again without my permission first. Do you understand?"

Teen: "Okay, okay, now can we look at the photo shoot?"

Parent: "Of course we will, when I'm done."

The teen rolls her eyes.

Parent: "Do you know why I feel this is dangerous?"

Teen: "Yeah, yeah, I know... Pedophiles, weirdo's, abductions, blah blah blah."

Parent: "Well, if you know this and you still chose to do it, what do you think I should do about it? After all, it's my job to keep you safe."

The teen looks at the parent, dumbfounded.

Parent: "I think until I can trust you again, the laptop will only be used in the kitchen or living room, okay?"

Teen: "Okay…"

Parent: "Thank you. Now that I feel better, let's look at that photo-shoot."

Whether you agree or disagree with the parent doesn't change the message. The teen understands the parent's expectations, is facing the consequences of their choice, and the lines of communication are open. The parent is staying calm, being honest about their feelings, and holding the teen accountable for their actions.

Marilyn Monroe once said, "Sometimes when things fall apart, they are actually falling into place," and just remember, in both the good times and the more challenging times, this too shall pass. I've taken much solace in these words. As a parent, you are learning more about yourself and nothing will teach you faster than a teenager. Remember to keep putting each situation into perspective; detach and stay calm. This is their journey...you are simply a guide.

Again, we live in a new world of entitlement, where you deserve everything without sacrifice. There is no requirement of worth and no consequences for mistakes. The youth have been told their life has a "no fail" policy and that everybody gets a ribbon, but we know this isn't truly how the world works.

I have heard parents talking about Santa Clause. Some people believe it is wrong to lie to your child about the myth of this jolly fat guy spreading gifts throughout the world, and they feel that the lie will ultimately hurt the child later and lead to resentment. I'm not here to debate Santa Clause and whether or not this is a good practice for you. Personally, this was one of my favorite parts of being a parent. But it does raise an interesting question... If we keep telling our children they "deserve everything" (which is completely different than saying they can "achieve anything"), are we setting them up for success or for failure?

Unfortunately, the independence rate of our youth is becoming older and older with each passing year. According to Human Resources and Skills Development Canada, young adults are delaying their transition from the parental home. Between 1981 and 2006, the proportion of young adults aged 20 to 29 who resided in their parental home rose 16 percentage points, from 27.5% to 43.5%.

The US is experiencing the same outcome. Some of this is due to the economic states of both countries, and some to the reasons children leave home. Mostly it is due to a lack of coping skills for making it in a world outside of school. Yes, there are challenges finding employment, securing careers, and affording the costs of living, but mostly there are consequences outside the home; there are decisions to be made, and there is a need to prove your worth. Our youth are largely ill-equipped for the task.

You can break this cycle with your teen, but it won't be easy for you. In fact, this will be one of the most challenging and important steps you will ever take as a parent. Parents have a desire to ensure their offspring doesn't have to endure the same hardships they did. They want their child to be successful, to get there with ease, and to find happiness. For many parents, their success or failure as a person depends on it. If this sounds like you, take some time to sit with it.

If you protect and guide them through every step they take, your teen will be left frustrated and without an understanding of why they aren't entitled to everything they want and why they are expected to prove themselves. They will want to be treated and trusted as an adult, but have not earned this designation and will not understand why this is required. Even if they enter adulthood and things go smoothly under your guided direction, what is going to happen at the first major life obstacle? Will they have the necessary learned skills to cope?

Your child deserves to grow as a person through challenges and hardship. If you want your child to become a functioning, independent and productive part of society, you have a responsibility to allow them to fail and face the consequences of their choices. This is your choice to make.

10 MANAGER MANUAL

Before we can explore how to incorporate defusing drama in the workplace, we first need to build a relationship with the employees. This new generation looks at the authority line differently than past generations. They view their employers in the same way as they did their teachers, parents and counselors. These people were in their lives to help and support them. They've never existed in a world that was guidance-free.

Your position as a supervisor, manager or leader will require this element of guidance, and will be quite effective if you first take the time to build a professional relationship with your employees. This will require them to trust that you are facilitating the right environment for them to learn, grow and feel appreciated. With these three aspects firmly in place, you will be ready to have the necessary conversations and they will be receptive to your input.

Many young adults lack the skill of providing face-to-face service, as they are a generation surrounded by technology: texting, networks and web access. They shop online, socialize accordingly, and prefer self-checkouts to cashiers. The service industry is being really challenged to meet the needs of this generation, while supplying service-skill oriented employees for the previous generations.

For many of today's millennials, jobs are not a priority or something to be kept in balance with the rest of their life, as with other generations. Life is priority, and work needs to accommodate their social life. They start out by saying that they will work around what the business needs, but later change their stance to reflect their calendar or habits.

This generation wants to feel that they contribute to the organization in which they are employed, and they want to take pride in their company. They want to develop, grow and feel their managers are invested in them; but with millennials, you as an employer have a crucial role in finding balance. The current generation is motivated quite differently than past generations, and managers across North America are now changing their management style to facilitate this.

You give your new employee their job description and, once you are confident they understand their role, you assume they will fulfill their obligations. In the beginning, your new employees will perform the job as laid out to the best of their ability, but very quickly their performance declines. Why?

First: You have to understand that your new employee is all about networking, so they will quickly begin to reflect what your other employees find important and unimportant. Monkey see, Monkey wants to belong, Monkey "not" do.

Second: Your employee waited for you to praise them on the job they were doing, and when that praise didn't come, they felt it was unimportant and discontinued. I can hear your manager thoughts now: "You mean I have to praise them for doing their job?" The short reply to this is YES! In past generations, a pat on the back for doing something within their job description would be taken as an insult. Today, however, this is a necessary requirement for the employee to continue the desired behavior.

If you give your employee an abundance of recognition, they will continue the behaviors they were recognized for. They will feel good about themselves, enjoy their work, and take pride in their job...but beware...eventually, since they feel they are doing such a good job (because you told them they were), they will start to feel they are more entitled than the next new hire to a promotion, to pay increases, to the best shifts and to more recognition. When this doesn't happen, resentment will ensue.

Now, there is also a need for performance management. When coached to change behavior, your employee will listen and adjust their performance to match the given expectation. To increase your success with your feedback, ensure your employee is given the "why" behind selected policies; they then will have an increased "buy in" to continue this behavior, even in your absence.

Again, beware – they will see that others are being held to the same accountability, they will talk amongst themselves, and they will either point out faults or start performance-managing others around them. With constant critical feedback, their self-esteem will crumble and they will either take on a position of superiority when someone else is in trouble, or they will become disengaged from the company and will leave your employment.

Development is a great strategy for keeping employees engaged. Teaching them a new skill will definitely do that if they feel the skill you're teaching will somehow benefit them. It may be that the new skill tells them you have faith in them, you want to invest in them, or that it's necessary for career advancement. Development will not only increase their skill set, but it will also increase their investment in your company.

But again, beware – if they want to develop and then they are never properly trained, or fail and are left without the support to learn from those mistakes, the employee will become discouraged and either give up or disengage from the company. Failing is not something this generation is equipped to handle. In their world, everyone got a ribbon. So set smaller, achievable goals in your development strategy. This will keep your employee motivated and confident.

When your employee is given an opportunity for a possible leadership position, they will be highly driven and motivated but will also have an expectation that you will guide and direct them with each step. As an employer, this can be very time-consuming and draining, and you have a business to run that requires your full attention. You want them to succeed, but you need them to become free-thinkers, self-motivated and self-driven.

First make sure you are facilitating an environment that allows people to make mistakes without fear or judgment. This generation doesn't like to fail, and they haven't had the experience with it that previous generations have. If your employees embrace an environment that enables them to learn that there will be mistakes, you can be successful with your task.

For a successful development plan, you must first lay out these guidelines:

- This is why you have been selected
- This is the expectation for the next step
- This is the behavior/skill we are looking for
- You will need to drive this yourself
- Be comfortable making mistakes
- Reassess your plan/progress regularly
- You must track your results
- I will be here for support and questions, but I won't give you the answers
- Set a follow-up date to review progress and celebrate successes

Ensure they know where to locate any necessary resources, and ensure that when you see them in action you are providing the recognition and feedback that will keep them driven and motivated. Set a follow-up date –

be sure to assess your employee when making this decision, as some work better with a set date given to them, while others need the flexibility to choose the duration.

Ensure they understand you are going to help them by giving them any tips on how to better their results before your next meeting. During this follow-up, let them deliver their progress report, telling you about their challenges and their successes. You can probe with open-ended questions to guide the conversation (think of it like an interview). Once they are done, provide them with "supportive" feedback. It's important they feel you are in their corner, wanting them to succeed.

- I would have worded this like ____________________.
- I really like how you ____________________________.
- I think what you are trying to say is _____________________.
- Fantastic _____________________________________.
- If ____________ didn't work, what might be a different tactic?

This is very much a two-way conversation: a collaboration on direction, time frame, and "next" steps. At this point, it is important that they know what they need to do to be successful, and they need to see the finish line as they are driven by short term goals. As this generation is motivated by instant gratification, short-term goals are incredibly important; anything that drags out too long will quickly demotivate them.

The key to this new generation is balance. I, as the manager/supervisor, have to regularly take notice and recognize what they are doing well (especially behaviors in the basic job description). I also need to manage any behaviors I want improved and be ready to coach and develop new skills. As the employer, you are a master juggler, and this fact has never been as prominent as it is today. Your employee does want to do a good job. They want to know what they can improve on and they want to continuously learn...their way! You must ensure you are providing an equal amount of recognition, feedback, and opportunity for development. If any of the three are lacking, your juggling balls will become unbalanced and your act will bounce on the curb.

This new way to look at management takes a completely different mindset, a great deal of patience, and a willingness to put your energy into your people differently. As this new business environment unfolds, it is also important to know how to manage these employees in the world of "choices and "boundaries." To be successful at this, I hope you as a manger have first done your own work on emotional detachment, as you are about to be tested.

We have already established that our role with these new employees is different than in the past, but this change extends out to the employee. They usually job-hop every year-and-a-half, and as a manager you know how costly this can be with the expense and investment of training, the impact to your business, and your personal state of Zen. However, there is good news: if your employees want to work for you, they will stick around much longer, and even if they do explore other career options, many times they will return to you.

Just like everything else with this generation, it's all about balance. Your goal is to ensure your employees feel a personal connection with you, and at the same time recognize you have a job to do which will not be compromised. If you are on "friendship" terms with an employee, they may feel they should be treated differently, just as you may find it harder to uphold performance management. If you are a "black and white" manager, where there is only the "right way and the wrong way" for employees and management to interact, your employees won't find that personal connection to you and will disengage. You must first, as a manager, know who you are and be comfortable in your own skin. You must be willing to be vocally honest, without emotion or judgment. Stick with the facts and offer choices in your conversations.

As an example:

A manager comes across one of their employees crying.

Manager: "Hey, are you okay?"

The employee just shakes their head.

Manager: I'll give you a few minutes, as I know a bit of space always helps me emotionally. I'll come back and check on you.

Once you have returned, LISTEN! Verbally replay the situation you have heard and how it has affected your employee.

Manager: "Wow, so after 25 years your parents are splitting up, and you're finding your current home life unbearable with both parties unloading on you."

The employee nods their head in agreement.

Manager: "So, what are your choices?"

The employee just stares back, like the manager has grown two heads.

Manager: "Let me help you get started…"

1) You could leave home

2) You could tell both parents it's not fair that they both are using you to sling mud

3) You could try to fix their marriage

4) You could take a social work course

5) You could be miserable every day

6) You could go to all your friends and vent

7) You could go talk to a counselor

8) You could call a lock smith

Some of these options will be funny, as they are either exactly what they are doing or something that would never be an option. The choices are endless.

Manager: "So which of these choices are NOT an option?"

Employee: "Number three."

Manager: "You're right... You can't fix this for them, just like I can't fix this for you! I'm not qualified!"

After removing more choices from the list, they may decide on an option or be down to only a few choices. Either way, they're on the right track and should have found their composure by now! Now it's time to talk about NOW.

Manager: "So I understand what you are going through, and you know that I have to run a business, so I need you to make one more choice. I need you to leave your situation in the back here – it will be here for you to pick up when you leave – put on the face I need for our customers, and come back out on the floor. If you don't think you are able to detach yourself from this right now, just let me know so we can send you home!"

Step one...getting them to look at choices which empower them.

Step two...the power of choice.

Step three...work choice.

Did you notice that the employee is making the choices? The manager is only the guide! The manager is being unemotional but supportive, and still maintaining a personal boundary with clear expectations.

Are you thinking that you don't have time for that kind of a conversation? My only answer to you is MAKE THE TIME! If you want to retain employees from this generation, have them exceed and positively impact your business and the experience of your customers, then you'll make the time!

Let's look some other examples:

Employee: "I'm having a hard time today. I might need to go home."

Manager: "Let's take five so you can tell me what's going on."

The employee proceeds to tell the manager of their recent break up, and the legal action that is now in progress over some disputed bills.

Manager: "Hmm, no wonder you're upset, separation disputes are never easy and sometimes quite messy."

Employee: "I know, I can't stop thinking about it, even at work, and now her new boyfriend is involved and my parents..."

Manager: "I understand your predicament. So what are you going to do?"

Employee: "What can I do?"

Manager: "Well...you do have some choices. You can continue to dwell on what you can't change, you can keep giving this situation power over you, you can trust the legal process, you could be grateful for the support network you have, you could burn all your belongings... What other choices do you have?"

With guidance, the employee lists off some more options.

Manager: "So, what are you going to do?"

The employee picks out a few choices, then starts to formulate a plan.

Manager: "So what would be the outcome or consequence of these few choices?"

The employee lists some potential outcomes.

Manager: "Well which one do you choose?"

After some deliberation, the employee picks an option.

Manager: "Doesn't it feel better when you feel you have some control over the situation? We have an employee assistance program; I'm going to give you the number in case you feel you need some help or guidance."

Employee: "Thank you."

Manager: "Do you think you are ready now to go back to work? I need you on your A game, so I need to know that if you go back on the floor, you're in the right mindset."

Employee: "I know. I've got this."

The more of these REAL conversations you have, the tighter the bond will become with your employees. These are also opportunities for enlightenment, as these are powerful new skills they have obtained, and they have done it without excessive input or emotion.

Consider this next example:

Employee: "I'm sorry, but I need to give my notice."

Manager: "Oh okay, what will you be doing now?"

The employee explains about a grand new opportunity.

Manager: "May I ask you a question?"

The employee hesitates.

Employee: "Sure."

Manager: "When I hired you, I noticed you had a new job every 8-9 months. We had just talked about promoting you to the next position, and I thought you had found something worth sticking with for a while. If this isn't the right fit, I completely understand. My question is... What are you looking for?"

Employee: "I'm not sure. I've never thought of it like that before."

Manager: "Well then, I'm glad I asked the question. From an employer's position, seeing short-term employment repeatedly can harm your resume. Knowing this, I would suggest making your next employment stop something that you can stay at for a longer period of time."

Employee: "I had no idea employers looked at that."

Manager: "Anyways, it's been great having you here, and to put in your notice this is what you'll need to do..."

An employee, regardless of whether or not they intend to stay, should leave the company feeling they have learned, grown, and been supported. This manager really knew their employee and their background well enough to have this conversation. The employee in question came back the next day and, instead of giving their notice, stayed and did more soul-searching for about another year, and then started a new career with a clear direction for her future.

This is not the outcome for most exit conversations; however, if an employee comes back to a company, it's because of their relationships there. They refer their friends and family for the same reason. If you want a steady flow of applications and customers, invest in your relationships with your employees.

This is a very new management style, and differs greatly to those of the past. If you have been a successful manager for years, but all of a sudden find that the tactic you have used in the past is no longer getting the same results, then it's time that you make a change. If you are a millennial manager/supervisor, you must resist the temptation to give your opinion and just facilitate the process to empowerment.

I promise you that if you are able to build a relationship where they know that you value them, trust that you'll hold them accountable, and feel you are invested in their development, you'll get the results you need from your team and remove a great deal of unnecessary work drama. If you then empower these young adults to make independent choices, you and your mentorship will always be remembered and your lessons will be life changing.

WORD FUEL

WEBSTER'S DICTIONARY

Will (noun)

- The power of choosing; the faculty or endowment of the soul by which it is capable of choosing; the faculty or power of the mind by which we decide to do or not to do; the power or faculty of preferring or selecting one of two or more objects.
- The choice which is made; a determination or preference which results from the act or exercise of the power of choice; a volition.

Volition

- The act of willing or choosing; the act of forming a purpose; the exercise of the will.
- The result of an act or exercise of choosing or willing; a state of choice.
- The power of willing or determining; will.
- The act of willing the act of determining choice, or forming a purpose. There is a great difference between actual volition, and approbation of judgment. Volition is the actual exercise of the power which the mind has of considering or forbearing to consider an idea.

Choice

- Act of choosing; the voluntary act of selecting or separating from two or more things that which is preferred; the determination of the mind in preferring one thing to another.
- The power or opportunity of choosing.
- Choice consists of the mental process of thinking involved with the process of judging the merits of multiple options and selecting one of them for action.

Power

- Ability to act, regarded as latent or inherent; the faculty of doing or performing something; capacity for action or performance; capability of producing an effect, whether physical or moral.
- Power (sociology), the ability to make choices or influence outcomes, which is also power held by a person or group of people in a society.

54001427R00042

Made in the USA
San Bernardino, CA
05 October 2017